The
Flame Lily Weeps

The
Flame Lily Weeps

Dr. Ross Gordon Cooper

PNEUMA SPRINGS PUBLISHING UK

First Published in 2009 by:
Pneuma Springs Publishing

The Flame Lily Weeps
Copyright © 2009 Dr. Ross Gordon Cooper
ISBN: 978-1-905809-53-0
Edition 2

Pneuma Springs Publishing
A Subsidiary of Pneuma Springs Ltd.
7 Groveherst Road, Dartford Kent, DA1 5JD.
E: admin@pneumasprings.co.uk
W: www.pneumasprings.co.uk

A catalogue record for this book is available from the British Library.

CONTENTS

DEDICATION

To my courageous family whose hearts belong in Zimbabwe.

To all the innocent blood that has been spilt in my country.

To the re-birth of a new Zimbabwe.

Flowers in Harare Botanical Gardens

Pomona Vlei, Harare

ACKNOWLEDGMENTS

I wish to thank my parents and extended family for very kindly reading through sections of the manuscript and making useful comments, and providing some supporting material. No man is an island!

Teviotdale Road, Harare

Harare garden flowers!

PERSONAL QUOTATION

Advice on selecting one's opportunities wisely

One has to determine the long-term value of an opportunity that presents itself. This can be related to the following story:

A baboon is presented with two maize cobs, one short and one long one. The baboon snatches the long cob without thinking. This is similar to what an unwise person does. In this case, one should look first at the size of the grain seeds before grabbing what appears to be the biggest meal. The short cob has larger, tastier seeds; with this one should seek to determine the long-term gains of a situation, rather than doggedly stepping into an area that looks initially attractive, but might very well have nasty repercussions.

By Ross Cooper, 1996

Devil's Cataract, Victoria Falls

Main Falls, Victoria Falls

Crocodile Farm, Victoria Falls

POEM

I came to London to see the world.
And what did I see?
I saw the me!
Running about like a bug;
No time for a mug.
Eat my crisps in pain,
I don't know why I'm trying again!

Let me lean on this wall, because, damn, I'm very tall!
My back is so sore, must be because I'm poor.
Spent a fortune on a house, makes me feel a mere mouse!

Now I've time for two mugs,
No longer feel like a bug!
Can eat my crisps without pain;
No need to try again!
Poverty is no more;
Cause I can go to the store.
Do not need a wall; I've come to the mall,
By car, no fuss, don't need the bus!

By Ross Cooper, 2006

Railway bridge, Victoria Falls

PREFACE

The iridescent petals of the flame lily (Liliaceae, *Gloriosa superba*) bespeak of the beauty of the so-called Dark Continent, Africa, the multitude and abundance of wildlife and plants in all their splendour and glory. Its petals resemble dancing warriors clad in colourful tunics impressively displayed in the hot sun, symbols of a proud, indomitable spirit.

Rhodesia, now Zimbabwe, had many unique black tribes (Anglo-African, Jews of Rusape, Manyika, Ndau, amaNdebele, maShona, Tswana and Vadoma) most of whom lived in harmony with the White, Indian and Coloured (mixed race) peoples. The country boasted the rugged Chimanimani mountains; the splendid rock formations in Matopos; the glorious Victoria Falls; Wankie (now Hwange) game reserve; Inyanga (now Nyanga); bushmen rock paintings at Domboshawa and Matopos; Birchenough Bridge and the Sabi (now Save) river; the Zambezi River and Lake Kariba; the Zimbabwe Ruins; Ewanrigg botanical gardens; the National Herbarium and Botanic Garden; Mukuvisi Woodland; amongst other sites. The country, named after its forefather, Cecil John Rhodes, was formed after the conquest of the tribes resident in Mashonaland and Matabeleland and, following the dissolution of the Federation of Rhodesia and Nyasaland (1953 – 1963), was named Southern Rhodesia (1964). It was, however, short-lived and was renamed Rhodesia that same year. Its economy, based principally on agriculture and exports of minerals, tobacco and beef, boomed creating a country that was named The Breadbasket of Southern Africa. Most citizens lived in relative prosperity and there was always plenty to go around. Peace was, however, not to last due to the growing sense of disenchantment chiefly amongst the black tribes over the apportionment of land and governance of the country. When Prime Minister Ian Douglas Smith of the Rhodesian Front declared Unilateral Declaration of Independence (UDI) on 11 November 1965, black nationalists (Zanu and Zapu) decided to embark on a bloody civil war, which cost thousands of lives.

The beauty of the flame lily, portrayed in its six reflexed, wavy red petals, often yellow marginated with long, protruding stamens, were

11

certainly reasonable motivators to classify it as the national flower of Rhodesia. All parts of the plant including the rootstock, however, are highly toxic if ingested due to the colchicine content. Indeed, the beauty of this country was irradiated not without a bitter pill, a poignant symbol of the price of betraying one's trust.

As a boy, I grew up in Africa, in my beloved country, exposed to nature in its essence and purity, and the exquisite beauties of its flora and fauna. An extremely creative and interesting mind was undoubtedly moulded in my search to explore the hidden secrets of nature. I liked wandering about the garden and collecting all sorts of insects, spiders, animals and plants to take home and show my parents. As a young child, I would frequently greet my Grandfather with a handful of pebbles gleefully shouting, "Look Grandad! Look what I've got for you!" My family was indeed encouraging of a creative mind and spirit. My father threw himself into his veterinary career and hobbies including the first, complete Rhodesian butterfly collection. My mother perfected her domestic and social skills and we were never without a meal on the table. My inseparable brother, Jason, accompanied me everywhere. As an adult, I regarded myself as a son of the soil, a true patriot of Africa – a part of its majestic peoples, a being of nature and the sun. Yes, indeed, I was one of the flame lily petals, proud and imaginative. The air was warm and filled with the chorus of Christmas beetles, bees and birds, its scent pervading all recesses of my keen mind. The chatter of people, the barking of dogs and the calls of game heralded our fame and that we were all happy. But, like a chill wind, suddenly a sharp crack of a round discharging, a chatter of machine gun, the roar of a Hyena (an armoured vehicle), a howl of a Vampire (jet fighter), the drone of a Lynx (turboprop fighter), and the whap-whap of a Alouette (attack helicopter) were heard. I was confused! Why were our peoples fighting? The beautiful flame lily petals were like drops of blood. They had been bitten and chewed and the poison in them released. I had been born into the throws of a civil war. A war bent on the elimination of colonialism and the establishment of black, majority rule. A dark cloud had descended upon my beloved country! A cloud so dense and foreboding that its mass extended, unchallenged for decades to come. The war and post-independence violence brought great fear, insecurity and disappointment to millions of Rhodesians and then Zimbabweans. All we sought was to live in peace.

Topographical map of Zimbabwe

This autobiography describes my life in Rhodesia, Zimbabwe-Rhodesia and subsequently after the attainment of independence on 18th April 1980, in Zimbabwe, and, thereafter, my move to and settling in the UK. It is not meant to be an exhaustive, family, historical or political account. Instead, it was born from a desire to reveal and elucidate the perspectives of a down-to-earth, white African boy living a life-time in Zimbabwe, and to tell the true story about certain poignant issues in the country's transition from a British colony to an independent, one-party state.

Geographical map of Zimbabwe showing principal towns and cities

1

THE ORIGINS OF MY FAMILY

My Grandparents, the Coopers, met and married during Adolf Hitler's scourge of Europe in a small town, Southgate, in the Borough of London (1940). My Grandfather, Gordon Thompson Cooper, classically wore his khaki military attire with sergeant stripes adorning his sleeve on the big day. My Grandmother, Eva Lillian Horrod, seven years his senior, descended from a two-child humble working class background in Hackney, London, the daughter of a London tube driver. It is probable that their names, Eva and Vera, were reflective of a then socialist workers view, although later in life, Mr. Horrod became quite conservative politically. Before he joined the London Underground, he was apprenticed to a blacksmith, working in a smithy with horses. As driving a tube was essential employment, he was not sent to the trenches, and thus survived the First World War, unlike two of his brothers.

The Cooper family, Southgate, UK. My grandfather Gordon Cooper is in the front centrally sitting on the ground

Marriage of Gordon and Eva Cooper

Just married – Gordon and Eva Cooper

**The two united families (Horrods and Coopers)
and friends celebrate**

My grandfather enlisted in the British Army on 16th March 1940. The Second World War brought many challenges and, although separated for lengthy periods, the marriage of Gordon and Eva was strengthened in absence. From this union, two sons were born, Richard (1942) and John (1946). After a rather unceremonious discharge from the forces, my Grandfather took up employment in a mechanical workshop progressing through the ranks to shop foreman. He was a product of a large, extended family, indeed one of seven children and it was hard for him to consider leaving the country the freedom of which he had fought for so bravely for six years in Italy and North Africa. My Grandfather attained the final rank of Sergeant (acting) (service number 2007486) serving with the Royal Engineers (13th March – 30th September 1942) and the Royal Electrical and Mechanical Engineers (1st October 1942 - 17th June 1946). He left the Army with numerous service medals (1939-45 Star - Battle of Britain; Africa Star – 1st Army; Italy Star; Defence Medal – Silver laurel leaves; and War Medal 1939-45 – Oak Leaf).

The economic hardships in post-war England and the inspiration of my Grandmother's sister, Vera, added fuel to the gate-keeper fire and dominant Grandmother, that resulted in the decision to move and settle in Africa. Gordon had originally been introduced to Eva through Vera's boyfriend Cyril whilst on a double date. Eva was very close to her sister, and with her father, Mr. Albert Edward Horrod, living in Cape Town as well, she probably felt the need to immigrate to be closer to them both. Cyril of course had travelled to numerous places during his service in the Merchant Navy and this may have provided the impetus to immigrate to Cape Town.

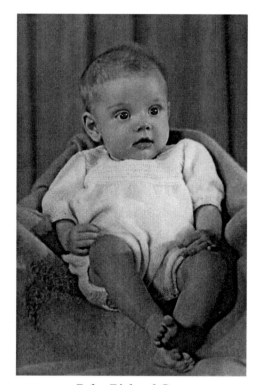

Baby Richard Cooper

Richard Cooper 5½ years old

The happy Cooper family with two sons, Richard and John

My father was born at Well House Hospital in Middlesex. The family lived at 104 Osidge Lane until 1944. My father kept a rabbit which he named Harold. The garden had a swing in the back and a wooden fence in the front, often a source of irritating splinters. He remembered the blackouts, air raid sirens and a bomb falling in Osidge Lane. During the war, food rationing was notoriously unpopular. Gordon was away at war in Algeria, Italy and France. The family moved to a one-room flat in Renelagn Gardens, Southgate for the duration of the war, followed by a move to 107 Osidge Lane. At this residence my father lived with his parents and maternal grandparents often paying visits to his Aunty Dot and paternal grandmother at 56 Lowther Drive, Enfield. Whilst resident at this address, my father attended pre-school at the local church hall in 1946 located near Hampden Square in Southgate. This was followed by Southgate Primary School until Grade Four. He distinctly remembers his teachers by name: Miss. Tight, Mrs. Gansler and Mr. Robinson.

My Grandfather had fortuitously been offered a job in Duly's motor company in Cape Town as a salesman. With little in hand and possessions packed into four wooden trunks, they departed UK in April 1953 on a steam liner to the Union of South Africa. The excitement of the journey, however, diluted any misgivings and the family eagerly threw themselves into the various entertainments offered on board, my father winning a fancy dress competition for the most unusual hat – a paper elephant. They were surprised somewhat when they entered a system fairly hostile to English-speakers, an Afrikaner-dominated society that harboured unforgiveness and bitterness from their alleged miss-treatment in British concentration camps during the Boer War. My Grandfather's apparent inability to learn Afrikaans resulted in many difficulties, including termination of employment and subsequent survival on income from odd jobs. The die had been caste for their departure from South Africa, and, fortunately, my Grandfather successfully applied for an advertised position as a salesperson in Duly's Motors in Umtali (now Mutare), Southern Rhodesia. To the family's delight, the managing director offered them paid transport for their train fares and furniture to settle in a house provided by the company. The family immigrated to Southern Rhodesia in April 1954 in a town located in one of the most picturesque parts of the country, the Eastern Highlands. In South Africa my father attended Claremont Primary School for Standards Four and part of Five, followed thereafter by enrolment into Standard Five at Chancellor Junior School and Umtali Boys' High School in January 1955 until December 1961. His brother, John Cooper, enrolled into Chancellor Junior School (1955-8) and then Umtali High (1959-64).

Richard Cooper aboard a liner destined for South Africa

Richard and John, Umtali 1957

The family lived initially in Mercury Mansions, followed by a rented house at 4 Stevens Avenue, Morningside. My father spent the majority of his school holidays in Mozambique camping and collecting butterflies – one of his many hobbies. After A-Levels, he worked for the Rhodesian Wattle Company and at Duly's and Co. in Umtali (1961-2). He then took a temporary job at the Pig Industry Board outside Salisbury (now Harare) as a Research Farm Assistant. His main form of transportation was a 500cc Norton motorcycle. Following a successful application, he was awarded a full bursary by the Rhodesian government for a five year degree study in Veterinary Science at the University of Pretoria. He passed every examination apart from virology, which he re-sat and passed in February 1968 and attended graduation in April 1968 in the presence of his parents and his girlfriend, who later became my mother. Thereafter, he worked as a locum in Johannesburg and Nelspruit in South Africa. In April 1968, he flew by Trek Airways from Johannesburg via Luanda, Cairo, Malta and Luxembourg to London. He stayed with his Aunty Dot and worked as a locum in Newport, Wales, Ascot, Windsor, Maidstone in Kent, and The Isle of Sheppey for the remainder of the year. He returned to Rhodesia in 1969, joined the Rhodesian government and was subsequently based in Salisbury until 1973. Whilst practicing as a Government Veterinary Officer he wrote and published in 1973, a Bundu Book, a subsidiary of Longman Rhodesia entitled, "Butterflies of Rhodesia" - the first of its kind and which has been used by avid insect collectors ever since, currently being marketed as, "Butterflies of Zimbabwe". He was promoted to Assistant Provincial Veterinary Officer in 1974 and transferred to Chipinga covering Melsetter, Chisumbanje and Cashel Valley. In 1977 he was heavily involved with containing a severe foot- and-mouth outbreak amongst cattle. Following the separation of my parents, he transferred to Gwelo (now Gweru) in 1978. This trip was, however, short-lived and he resigned after four months and bought a private practice in Bulawayo in July 1978 which he still operates today. Initially, he lived in the surgery as it was basically a reconverted three-bedroom house. In December 1978 he bought a large, double-storey house (with 6 toilets!) at 5 George Avenue, Kumalo. My father remarried and had four children, one of which died in early infancy. He indulged himself in numerous hobbies and activities including the establishment of a massive vegetable patch. My brother and I always found something interesting to do at his house. He took up running in 1986 and triathlon events in 1987. Since then, he has successfully completed 11 Comrades and two Two Oceans marathons. He ran a gruelling 100km Standard Bank race in Harare in 1992, and in 2002, completed a 100 mile run in Cape Town. He currently runs 5 km every morning, often with his dog at heel.

Jason Cooper seconding his father on the 100km Standard Chartered Bank run, Zimbabwe, 1992

Richard Cooper vaccinating police dogs, Bulawayo, 2006

Grandparents happily retired, Mabelreign, Harare, 1989

The Eve of my Grandparent's 50th Wedding Anniversary, Harare

My mother's parents, the Nettmanns, grew up and attended school in a largely segregated South Africa. They met and married in Boksburg, Transvaal (now Gauteng) in 1948. My Grandfather, Cornelius Rademeyer Nettmann, named after his pioneer German Grandfather, worked as an assistant miner followed by an apprenticeship as a fitter and turner. After successfully completing his apprenticeship, he was employed at Colgate Palmolive where, unfortunately, he nearly lost the sight in both eyes after a pipe bearing caustic soda to the soap-making plant, burst in his face. It was the timely intervention of his assistant who rushed him under running water in a shower that saved his sight. He was always very hard working and was eventually promoted to Aircraft Engineer following his employment at Voortrekkerhoogte, Pretoria, until his retirement. Of all his jobs, he liked this one the most. He was a pleasant, easy-going, man who listened to Country and Western Music. He was also a very good sportsman particularly at soccer and achieved Eastern Transvaal colours as a goal-keeper. He often joked that he would have gone on to become a Springbok, like his cousin, Gilbert Peterson, who was the Springbok soccer captain for eight years, except that he had observed his wife-to-be, Doris Laureen Moore, riding a bicycle in shorts and had fallen deeply in love with her, a "disease" he said he endured with much joy and heartache until his death in 2004. He also enjoyed cricket and it was nothing for him to set up wickets in the dirt road outside their house in the Northern suburbs of Benoni and play a game with his children. Before long, most of the fathers and boys in the street/neighbourhood would also join in to play! He relaxed by fishing, a pastime he also loved and was good at. He regularly packed tents, camping and fishing equipment, and would take his whole family fishing for the day or weekend. It was not unusual for the family to sleep on groundsheets under the stars. He was a humble, deeply-righteous man who loved God and creation. Uxorious by nature, he loved his family unconditionally. The economy at the time was reeling from the depression and the family were mostly impoverished being dependent on my Grandfather's income, which also supported his own parents for a time after his father was involved in a serious motorbike accident.

My Grandmother descended from the British Pioneer, Frank Duke Henderson, who was an Engineer-cum-Architect. She was meticulous and quite bright for her day, and was awarded her Junior Certificate (equivalent to a Form 3 School Leaver's Certificate). However, she and her twin sister, Gladys, were forced to get office jobs to help support the rest of the siblings. There were eight children in her family, the elder two having died previously from diphtheria. The two twins were, therefore, the eldest of the remaining six siblings. Strange to say, both their grandfathers met in a pub long before the union of the two families through their grandchildren. Cornelius

Senior could not speak English fluently, nor could Frank speak any German, yet they became the best of friends and could communicate mainly by using sign language. My Grandparents union gave birth to four children, Doreen Dorothy Louise (1949), Claude Richard (1951), Wilhelmus John (1952) and Corinne Felicity (1956). Initially, the family lived in Brakpan, then moved to Boksburg where my mother attended Martin Primary School, thereafter translocating to Northmead, Benoni, after buying a three bed-roomed house. The other children attended Rynfield Primary School followed by secondary education in Benoni High School. My mother enrolled in the University of Pretoria on an Occupational Health programme. Claude and Wilhelmus took up metallurgy trades, and Corinne trained as a sales person.

My mother, Doreen, described her life as helping around the house with the cleaning, cooking, sewing, knitting, reading and giving help to her siblings with their homework. She was also very involved with Girl Guides, which were an extension of the domesticity practised at home and the love of the outdoors, given to her by her father in the form of hiking, stalking and camping. Part of the service to the community was taken up by the SA Red Cross where she passed Advanced First Aid/Emergency Helper and Home Care exams. She also attended church and sang in the church choir. She was awarded the SA "Founder's Guide Award" (the highest achievement for a Girl Guide on a par with the former Queen's Guide Award) just before her sixteenth birthday (1965). She was made Head Girl, after the approval of the Headmaster, David Moffat, due to her achievement in Girl Guides, school sports, services in the library, and always setting a good behavioural example. She passed University Entrance Matriculation Exemption Certificate (1966) and was awarded a State Bursary to do a 3-year diploma course in Occupational Therapy (1967 - 1969).

It was whilst enrolled at the University of Pretoria, that she met Richard Cooper during an initiation ceremony of first year students at Onderstepoort. A man, seven years her senior and in his final year, became her very good friend. She also met Robert Stegmann, still hacking his third year of Medicine for the second time, having failed

My mother's brothers and sister

My mother receiving the Founder's Guide Award

his preceding two years twice before, well into her first year of training. Unfortunately, the relationship with the latter did not materialise and she immigrated to Rhodesia and was met by her husband-to-be, Richard Cooper. My mother has lived never to regret her decision and described it as coming to a land with fresh, warm, unpolluted, life-giving air. As her qualifications were not recognised in Rhodesia and that she was not nurse-trained, she later embarked on a career as a Pre-School teacher for 6 years.

**My parents and aunt visiting the Balancing Rocks,
Epworth, Salisbury**

My parents marriage, Boksburg, South Africa

2

LIFE IN SALISBURY (NOW HARARE) (1970 – 1973)

I was born on the 23rd September, 1970 in Andrew Fleming Hospital, Salisbury. As a child, I remember my parents' marriage as a very happy one. They had lots of support and encouragement from my paternal Grandparents who paid regular visits and took it upon themselves to assist in the care of myself and my brother, Jason born in 1972. The Nettmann's never visited Rhodesia, although we did receive birthday and Christmas cards from them. I remember a life full of adventure in a large garden in Greendale suburb, Salisbury, with a swimming pool and trees, running about with Bentley the Alsatian cross and lots of friends. The pool had no filter and it was filled regularly with a garden hosepipe. My Grandmother would often pick me up and take me to visit her friends and to her voluntary work at the Red Cross. I remember, from an early age, my visits to their house in Mabelreign, Salisbury, the narrow, winding roads, the streetlights, the walks in the veldt and their well-kept garden abounding in fruit trees, aloes, cacti, flowers of all description, roses, poinsettias and deciduous trees. The Cyprus bush was a favourite haunt for hide and seek and my inseparable brother added excitement to games. We grew up surrounded by pets, two dogs Bentley and Tina, and Percy the tailless cat. The dogs were constantly following us about in every niché of the garden and were often seen whining at the cage housing guinea pigs and a monkey called Henry.

The days of Henry were, however, short-lived when my father was ordered to remove him from the property after a spate of cat chasing in the neighbour's house!

Baby Ross, Granny Eva and mother, Salisbury

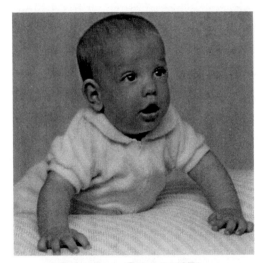

Baby Ross Cooper, 1971

Father and Ross Cooper aged 5½ months

Five generations – Great paternal Grandfather, Grandmother,
father and Ross Cooper

Great paternal Grandfather and Ross, Mabelreign, Salisbury

My brother, Jason, was born on the 5th September 1972 and I vaguely remember at the time being looked after by my Grandparents and snippets of his days as a screaming baby. He was born ill and could not properly digest meals with protein. He of course took over my cot (incidentally which my father made) adorned with effigies of white zebra and bush buck on a light blue background. My father, much like my Grandfather, was very creative with his hands and built many wooden toys and items of furniture for us children. My father also filmed us as we grew up and I have subsequently enjoyed many of the scenes, albeit without sound, growing up in Greendale and visiting Beira, Mozambique, Benoni, South Africa and Port Saint John, Transkei.

Ross peering through the gate of his Grandparents' house, Mabelreign, Salisbury

I regard myself as fortunate to have grown up with such a happy childhood spent mostly outdoors. As an innocent and naïve child, I was very surprised by the existence of our civil war, which Prime Minister Ian Douglas Smith described as a war against communist insurgents. In the early 1970s the cities were relatively immune from the bush war and it was only when my father received a transfer in 1974 to a small town on the Eastern border, Chipinga (now Chipinge), that I realised the full extent of the guerrilla campaign led by Robert Gabriel Mugabe's Zanu and Joshua Nkomo's Zapu against white-ruled Rhodesia. So it was with much excitement, albeit concern on the parts of my two sets of Grandparents, that Jason and I left wrapped in the back of a Ford Sierra station wagon with my parents to begin a new life in a town, Chipinga, where everybody knew each others' business - a town located perilously close to the Mozambique border and in an area ravaged by civil war. A town, though, blessed with numerous flame lilies!

Painting at Mukuvisi Woodlands tea garden, Harare

3

GROWING UP IN CHIPINGA (NOW CHIPINGE) (1974 – 1978)

Chipinga, located in the Melsetter district was originally bordered on the east by Mozambique, on the north and north-west by the Umtali district and west and south-west by the districts of Charter, Bikita and Ndanga, from which it was divided by the Sabi River. It occupied a total area of 800,000 ha, although it was later split up when the Chipinga district was formed, leaving only 310,000 ha remaining. The area consists of a series of broken plateaux of various altitudes, upon the central one of which the township of Melsetter was established. The land falls west and south, and the Chimanimani Mountains, with peaks rising to a height of about 2,450 metres (8,085 ft), form part of the Mozambique boundary. In the extreme south, the elevation is only 300 metres, being at the junction of the Save and Lundi rivers. The low country is somewhat stifling and humid, but elsewhere the climate is extremely salubrious.

Thomas Moodie of the pioneer column, on 3rd January 1893, halted at the green rolling hills of what became known as the Chipinga district. Present were three clear waterfalls, the spot where Thomas Moodie claimed his own farm, to which he gave the name 'Waterfall'. A town was soon built to support government, economic and business ventures, which grew into a thriving community boasting two Junior Schools, supermarkets, bottle stores, a town hall, a bakery, a public swimming pool, numerous industries and other concerns. We were settled in a house, 152 Moodie Street, which was let to the District Veterinary Officers at the time. The garden was extensive and had numerous fruit trees. The veldt ran the length of the property with a stream containing whirlpools that fed the municipal dam. It was teeming with wildlife, including duiker, bushbuck, porcupines, aardvark, aardwolve, jackals and snakes. Being exposed to such a variety of flora and fauna, I quickly learnt the names of each and was exceptional at answering nature questions in school.

I was soon to make many friends, four in particular, Karl Van Rooyen, Brendon Bridges, Gregory Isit and John Henry, with whom I spent many hours playing and exploring. Such antiques progressed to the more daring, beginning with catapults made out of old bicycle tubing and from thence onto pellet guns. By the time I was 6 years old, I had become quite a marksman. But this often got me into trouble especially when I would shoot paw paws, nartjies, oranges, bananas and window panes. I remember being chased by many an angry parent or worker brandishing a dreaded shambok (a whip made of a hippopotamus tail). I used to play the explorer in an extensive mielie (maize) patch and inspect the ripe corn by separating the tassels. I used to chew the seeds, which would exude a white chalky fluid. Unfortunately this patch lay adjacent to the chicken hoek (chicken house) and I inadvertently disturbed the rooster which attacked me with tremendous vigour causing me to run like the wind, screaming with the bird close at heel. This rooster was caught, killed and eaten. I was astonished to see its headless body running about.

At five I learnt to ride solo on a 20 inch rim bicycle and peddle everywhere boldly including the town centre, in spite of my father's disapproval. We used to show off by pegging a piece of card on the rim of the bike so that the spokes would make a crackling noise whilst rubbing against it. Twice this got me into trouble when I caught my flip-flops in the spokes whilst adjusting the peg, and ended up flying head first over the handlebars. Fortunately, neither my brother nor I were seriously hurt. The dogs were my constant companions and by this time, Bentley was seven. He used to get into a few scraps with other dogs but occupied most of his time sleeping under the snooker table or on the veranda. He would often stare for hours at the Chinchilla cage hoping that his luck would change and that he could catch one. I became close to the dog, as I believe he suffered a lot from billary (tick-borne) infections and loneliness. His life was unfortunately violently ended in a dogfight one night, and from thence on, Jason and I became attached to Present, a Labrador cross with a lame hind leg. He was to occupy our lives until 1987 when he was put down after developing incurable Hodgkin's lymphoma.

In 1974 I was sent to a crèche run by an old woman and I remember distinctly occupying most of my time playing outside. Only once did she call me in to identify a set of colours. I think that at this period of my life, my mind began to wonder and I longed for 1300 hr, that is, home time, so that I could go out into the garden with my friends. Fortunately, not long thereafter, in 1974, my mother established a pre-school and I joined that with much excitement and expectation. No favours were endowed on me, however, and I was treated just like any of the pupils. I learnt how to read, count, write, paint, play and have a good time. I met many of my friends during this time. I was baptised into the Anglican Church, St. Barnabas in Chipinga on 7th July 1974.

The Rhodesian government made it obligatory that once a child reached the age of five they should be enrolled into Junior School, starting in Kagi (Infants)-One (1975). I remember the day with trepidation, as I clearly abhorred the idea of being absorbed into a strange environment away from my home. In Chipinga Junior School I was soon coached in formal curricula, school uniforms, assemblies, compulsory sports and the like under the wings of Miss Mary Sheard (later Mrs. Carshalton whom I met again in 1995). She had waist length blonde hair and was very pleasant to us making us write in exercise books with a pencil. However, she did get angry, and was particularly upset when a couple of us were caught skidding on the wax-polished floor on the way to the boy's toilet, and also after spying on the visiting dentist. I, however, managed to stay hidden behind my chair, which we had to place on the desk just before home time, and escaped punishment. My school report revealed that I was an average pupil who could improve by concentrating more in class. I, however, excelled at science and was commended for a silkworm project. My father often used to drop me back at school for afternoon activities and, being shy of the Standard Five pupils whose classroom faced the car park, I would hide in the back of his Mercedes Benz motorcar. I was particularly fond of riding in the back of his Leopard, a high speed armoured and bullet-proof vehicle, but would feel embarrassed as it approached the school due to the powerful cacophony from its engine. I liked cross-country and excelled in Sports Day in the beanbag, sack and spoon races. Most of the pupils in my school were from farms and many of them spoke fluent Afrikaans. I grew to love the farming life and, although it was dangerous to travel along the roads, spent many a weekend on family farms. My mother befriended the Wilmse family and we would regularly accompany her on visits to the farm, famous for its two-storey house constructed as an ox-wagon. There was, however, a large element of bulling in the school and I was picked on because of my lack of physical strength and my big teeth. There was a blonde girl in Standard Five, however, who hit two bullies who were trying to throw me out of the milk queue, and, after that, I commandeered more respect. I wished later that I could thank that girl, but we lost contact when she went to Umtali Girls' High School the following year. We were issued stamps, the equivalent of ¼ cent, to either buy milk or caramel-flavoured milk at break time. We would eagerly do so and use this to wash down our sandwiches. Ice creams at the time were incredibly cheap, an iced lolly selling for ¼ cent. It was, indeed, a treasure to find one cent as that inevitably meant four lollies!

In 1976, I entered Kagi (Infants)-Two in the classroom next door and was taught initially by Mrs. Sheard, thereafter by a very nice Mrs. Dillane who insisted that all our bags be painted with our names and class. I was one of the last to do so, and remember having to surrender my satchel to her in the front for painting. Graeme Dillane, her son, commandeered the utmost respect, as we were scared he would report us to his father, the Headmaster! I was to meet him many years later whilst working in a fast-food takeaway, Chicken Inn, during my undergraduate studentship at the University of Zimbabwe.

Mrs. Dillane successfully got me to complete simple mathematical problems and I developed a flair for Art. I enjoyed the sessions at the back painting and making paper maché models. We were also required to attend once-a-month films shown in the school hall, thereafter writing a story about them. We usually started off with a cartoon and would watch them sitting cross-legged on the school hall floor. However, I rarely remembered what was shown thereafter and struggled to write a lengthy story about it. In one instance I got into trouble for copying Graeme. My end-of-year report, however, was more encouraging as it stated that I was making better progress and had a more positive approach to my work.

During lessons there was a strict, albeit unspoken requirement that only boys should sit together. We were required to cover our exercise books supplied by the Ministry of Education in brown paper and each textbook in plastic. For good measure, the school provided these resources. It was, however, an onerous task. Books were stacked neatly in our desks, which were often adorned with graffiti and carved names. There were also numerous ink blotches staining the wood, evidently from the days when school children were required to write with fountain ink. Ink wells and the grooves for fountain pens were etched into each desk. Often the well was a source of annoyance as it was through which sharpeners and rubbers disappeared. Pretentious students leaning over to say hello, would stuff sweet papers down the well holes. We were all well aware of the consequences of being caught with litter in our desks. Punishment usually included a brisk whack with a ruler across the hand. In the 1970s teachers were permitted to administer corporal punishment. Thankfully, I never received any of the like as I was usually a very obedient, quiet and applied student. There were regular offenders like John Henry and Karl van Rooyen, however, who were often called up for beatings.

My April 1977 report was usefully commented on by the Headmaster Mr. J. Dillane who noted that I had made satisfactory progress in all subjects during the term. My final school report for Infants (Kagi) – Two in December 1977 was nothing spectacular, although it was noted that I had made improvements in numbers, reading, writing and art work. The general comment on my report read, "Ross still lacks a certain amount of confidence in himself which is reflected in his work. However, he tries hard and is a willing and helpful member of the class". I was awarded two certificates for the Infants 2 Boys sack race (2nd place) and bean bag (4th place) on the 19th March, 1977. Looking back at my reports, it is weird and strange how teachers in those days regarded a quiet child as lacking in confidence and independence. In fact such an attitude would not be tolerated today as it is recognised that there is value in any child's demeanour as long as it steers away from the destructive. It is unfortunate that there was no section provided for sporting and extra-curricular activities in the Infant's Progress Reports. I suppose although I was outgoing and enjoyed life, I could have possibly spent a little more time studying.

The Standard One year was a graduation from and entry into a fresh phase of primary school. From this point onwards the progress report was tabulated into clearly designated areas: English (Spoken, Reading and Written), Mathematics, Content Subjects (History, Geography, Nature Study and Science), Art/Crafts, and other interests and games. It was impressive that the report featured the logo of the school which included Birchenough Bridge spanning the Sabi River containing the abbreviation, "CS", and circled by a rope of intertwined school colours, and the motto, "Per Laborem ad Honorem". In standard one our teacher, Mrs. A. Kotze was meticulous but could be strict and she used to discipline the particularly naughty boys with the end of a paint brush. Having visited the classroom years later I was amazed at how all of us 35 students managed to fit into the tiny room. The greater variety of activities meant that I began to work harder in Content Subjects and Art/Crafts.

Mrs. Kotze was the wife of an Afrikaner farmer. She had dark-brown hair and brown eyes, features reflective of French Huguenot ancestry. We were regularly reprimanded and given lots of homework. I felt as though my fun days at school had dissolved like a Disprin in a glass of water. I did, however, have some respite as Jason had enrolled in Infants (Kagi)-One. Reflecting on my experiences in her class years later, I believe she was one of our best teachers as she drove the need into us for hard work. I made good progress in all subjects and the comment in my April 1978 report for Art/Crafts was, "He works with care and has painted some good pictures". By December 1978, I was commended with the overall comment, "Ross has shown more interest in his work and in class activities this term. Well done Ross, keep it up".

Birchenough Bridge is located 62 km from Chipinge in the Manicaland province and links Mutare with Masvingo (then Fort Victoria). Completed in 1935 with funding from the Beit Trust, it reached a length of 329 m. In the 1970s a tare vehicle weight of 40 tons was imposed on the bridge. The bridge's road was widened in 1984 from 7.2 to 10 m and strengthened. Today the bridge is still considered as one of Zimbabwe's best architectural achievements. Unfortunately, due to the civil war it was deemed unsafe for school trips to see and study the bridge. We did get to observe the bridge, however, when travelling in a guarded convoy to Umtali.

The civil war in Rhodesia was escalating and the fear in citizens' hearts grew. At one stage there was a funeral every week in Chipinga as a consequence of KIA or murder. The usual guerrilla tactic was to plant a landmine or set up an ambush and once the deed was done, they melted back into the bush.

I was, 23 years later, to visit the graves of Chipinga residents killed in the war. They were all brave people and deserving of the highest accolade and respect. Whilst looking at their headstones, I wondered if all this blood shed had been necessary. Why was there all this hatred and uncertainty in the air? What were politicians doing? Our freedom had been taken away by the war and we dared not venture out of the relative safety of Chipinga town lest we get attacked. Convoys became obligatory, but not entirely safe either, one being severely attacked en-route to Umtali. Because of the threat of attack on our school, we had to practice attack drill lying flat on the classroom floor and racing into underground bunkers.

Call-up into the Rhodesian Army was compulsory for all males aged 18 and over. The Rhodesian Army also elicited the help of foreign soldiers from Britain, Canada, Denmark, Germany, New Zealand and the USA. The desire for independence from white minority rule saw the forced and voluntary taking up of arms by thousands of armed black guerrillas. There are many books written on the heroes of the hour and it is not the place of this book to repeat them. I did, however, constantly fear an attack. Many of my friend's parents had been killed. The mortaring of Chipinga town by guerrillas in 1978 was a cowardly act. We were sleeping in our beds and had to be rushed into underground bunkers. I remember the emergency siren howling long into the night. That night I was rudely woken by pounding feet and shouting! Chipinga town was being attacked and we all had to get into the bunkers as quickly as possible. I remember the troopers directing us underground and my brother's blanket dipping in pools of filthy water in the dark, musty corridors. The war had taken a new turn. Towns were now the targets. Ian Smith, PM had recently announced that black majority rule would be instigated within two years. Although there could have been a peaceful, power-sharing agreement reached amongst blacks and whites before UDI, Rhodesia had every right to defend its sovereignty and to protect its citizens from Marxist rule.

**A Rhodesian soldier who was awarded
the Grand Cross of Valour**

*Acting Captain C.F. Schulenberg, S.C.R. of the Selous Scouts was the first re-
cipient of the Grand Cross of Valour, Rhodesia's highest military medal. This
was followed by Major G. Wilson, S.C.R., B.C.R. who was second-in-command
of the Rhodesian SAS and Rhodesia's most highly-decorated soldier. This medal
was replaced in October 1980 by the Gold Cross of Zimbabwe.*

Grave of Rhodesian soldier Killed in Action, Chipinge

An amazing picture of a formation of Rhodesian Air-Force aircraft flying over Bangala Dam, Lowveld Irrigation Scheme, 30th October 1963. Shown are a Canberra 200 (front), a Vampire (T11 400) (rear), and two Hawker Hunters (sides) (courtesy of Mr. T. Chalmers)

I certainly improved in class throughout 1978 and my August report suggested a greater interest in my work and class activities and was complimented by my teacher. The new Headmaster was Mr Bowen. It was at this time that I was a boarder at Chipinga Junior School. I was deeply distressed at the prospect of being a boarder as I was separated from my mother - by now my parents were separated - and also from my brother. Year boarders were accommodated in different dormitories. Bullying, harassment and teacher intimidation was rife. The rigorous discipline of an enduring post-Victorian schooling system ensured that we were woken up at the crack of dawn, forced to make our beds in the most ridiculous of ways without a single crease or rumple, polish our shoes, have bed inspection, and then march into the food dormitory and sit on a bench in our standard. The food was basic, although filling, consisting of mielie-meal porridge, scrambled/boiled eggs, baked beans and bread. I disliked lunch as we were separated from non-border friends that we usually played marbles with and by the time we were asked to leave the dining hall it was the start of compulsory extramural activities. I liked swimming, playing soccer and engaged in athletics. By now a new swimming pool had been constructed at the school negating the need to use the municipal public baths. I joined Cub Scouts but the disarray and the violence therein meant that I did not last very long.

Dirt Road leading down to our house, Chipinge

Family home, Chipinge

Chipinge Primary School

Chipinge Hospital

Dutch reformed Church, Chipinge

The municipal baths I vividly recall were enormous, especially to my young mind, and I used to compete daringly after school by jumping off the 6 m diving board, although never head first. Dive bombing was a favourite. I believe that this was the first time that I established playful relationships with girls, and no better place than the swimming pool! Following swimming, we would romp down to the local store to buy chewies, Willard's chips, liquorice and peach-flavoured drops, the latter costing ¼ cents each. The delightful aroma of the Chipinga Bakery filled the air and I used to long to eat thick slices of freshly baked bread spread with copious amounts of Stork margarine and Sunlight jam. Money went a very long way and if I was in possession of a Rhodesian one-dollar note, I considered myself rich. A 300 ml bottle of Coca-Cola cost 10 cents including the deposit. I was given my first money bank from Barclays and saved a few coins, the most impressive and largest of which was the Rhodesian 25 cent.

Chipinge Sports Club

Rowing in Chipinga Municipal Dam

Chipinge Municipal Dam

51

Chipinge Municipal Offices

Parents were required to check and sign their child's homework, most of which I usually completed by 1700 hr. Following supper, I was in bed by 1800 hr. My mother served us copious amounts of salad, fresh vegetables and Rhodesian steak, the tastiest in the world. She used very little oil in her cooking and was a wizard at baking cakes. My father always said his favourite meal was a fried egg. Our eggs were collected every morning from our hoek (chicken house) and, being organic, were exceedingly rich and tasty. I liked a hearty breakfast of poached eggs, baked beans and black pudding. Tanganda tea stirred with heaps of brown sugar washed it all down. My father's tastes certainly extended to the exotic and he introduced me to fried flying ants (termites), chicken giblets and rooster sweetmeats (testicles).

Ross and Jason Cooper a-top a Leopard, Chipinga

Parked Leopard armoured vehicle, Chipinge

Birchenough Bridge, Chipinge

I was a very popular and outgoing child with lots of friends. I did miss my Grandparents though and we would really only see them once a year usually during visits to my Great Grandad, Mr. Horrod, in Fish Hoek, Cape Town. On the 16th February 1978, my Great-grandfather died and his executor, Cyril William Charles Lainson of 1 Naivasha, 1 Abbington Circle, Fish Hoek, Cape Town, had him cremated by Goodall & Williams (the undertakers).

I received numerous postcards from them most of which were typed up by my Grandmother on her typewriter. Our family seemed so happy and content. I spent a lot of time outdoors with the dogs and my pellet gun which my father bought for me for my sixth birthday. I used to shoot targets, aspiring to be a soldier, lizards and locusts, but no birds. Life was healthy and extremely enjoyable, devoid of the distractions of a television and cinema. We would accompany and go on adventures with the garden boy and indulged in playing with the maid's children who taught me how to make wire cars. My mother insisted that I develop an interest in cricket and we used to practice playfully in the garden. I collected numerous pictures of cricket players and glued them into my scrapbook. I also collected pictures of animals, cars and armoured vehicles. I certainly had inherited a very curious mind with numerous interests. My mother was later to comment fondly that she has never known somebody with as many interests as me.

Save River, Chipinge

Waterfall, Chipinge

Thomas Moodie's grave, Chipinge

Old Wilmse's farm house, Chipinge

View from Wilmse's farm house, Chipinge

Giant Rhodesian Mahogany, Chirinda Forest

4

MOVE TO SALISBURY (NOW HARARE) (1979)

Unfortunately, my parent's marriage soured and they separated in 1978. We were required to vacate the government veterinary house and move into a rented house further down the street on the corner of Moodie and 4th Street. My mother continued teaching nursery school there and we used to spend a lot of time with her friends. She befriended Ted Dawson the manger of Hugh Fennel's Chipinga coffee farm, "Crocodile Creek". I used to play with the farm dogs and in the tree house.

We moved to Salisbury in 1979 and settled in a one-room flat in Hatley House on North Avenue. My mother enrolled on a Book-keeping course at Speciss College and successfully passed her Pitman's examinations. Her furniture and assets were kindly stored on Mr. Fennel's farm and later transported to Harare when she secured a rented two bedroom flat at Jels Court in Avondale.

I was enrolled in Blakiston Junior School. My teacher Mrs. Horsfield was a nice brunette. School life in Salisbury seemed more competitive, although, on reflection I was behind in my school work due to the upheaval from my parents divorce. Our classroom's roof used to shake as Rhodesian Air force helicopters raced low overhead to land at Andrew Fleming Hospital, mostly carrying wounded soldiers, although wounded civilians were also cassevaked. During this year, the main oil depot in Southerton was attacked with tracers and Rocket Propelled Grenades (RPGs) and burnt for a whole week. Approximately half a million barrels of oil, which the embargoed Rhodesian government had painstakingly accumulated from Iran and South Africa, were destroyed. This disaster increased Rhodesia' budget deficit by 18% within a few minutes. The value destroyed was estimated to be at least a million times that expended in rockets and tracer bullets. It was frightening to realise that the guerrillas had successfully entered Salisbury. Fire fighters from South Africa were eventually recruited to quell the blaze. I remember the black smoke from the burning oil rising high into the clouds. This was a precipitant for the end of Rhodesia and the birth of Zimbabwe-Rhodesia under the new leadership of Bishop Abel Muzorewa.

On the 10th February 1979, the Herald newspaper printed a photograph of myself, Jason and two black teenagers, Moses Kalisa and Munyaradzi Marise rocking on the latest addition to the playground in Salisbury gardens, the super-rocker. This picture was intended to illustrate the transition from separation to integration, and to recognize that all men in Zimbabwe-Rhodesia were equal. It's a pity that Mugabe and Nkomo chose to continue the war, though, with the ultimate objective of the complete riddance of white rule. It cost the country many lives.

e Herald

Incorporating The Nation

SALISBURY, SATURDAY FEBRUARY 10 1979

Registered at the General Post Office as a newspaper.

Herald Reporter

LATEST addition to the playground in Salisbury Gardens is this "super rocker". And, as you can see, it's super fun.

The object of the exercise — and exercise it is! — is to bounce the other kids off and stay king of the castle. Demonstrating are brothers Jason (6) and Ross Cooper (8), Moses Kaliso (14), on the right, and Munyaradzi Marise (14).

Four Zimbabwe-Rhodesian boys heralding the birth of a new era!

61

5

SCHOOL AND LIFE IN HARARE (1980-1989)

After our move to Jels Court my brother and I were enrolled in Avondale Junior School. I preferred this school as it was more dynamic and I began to excel academically and in sport. I remember being given a reading test by the big bearded be-speckled Headmaster, Mr. Cracknell. We nicknamed him Crack-a-Jack because of his fondness for beating with a cane. I was taken back to class Standard 5M from my first assembly by a very kind and sweet Miss Kennedy for the first two terms in 1980 and subsequently replaced by Mrs. Grundy in third term. General remarks on my December 1980 report were, "Ross is rather reserved in oral work, but has a pleasant nature and tackles all work with determination". I developed a flair for tennis and insisted on playing regularly in the beginners' team every Wednesday afternoon. By this time Zimbabwe-Rhodesia had transitioned into independent Zimbabwe on the 18th April 1980. I felt a sense of relief that the war was now over.

My year in Grade 6M, 1981, saw a remarkable improvement in my work and I achieved mostly A grades. My teacher Mrs. Noel commented on my research work as being excellent and that my books were beautifully maintained. I guess that this was the time when the making of a researcher was born. I attained first position in class and was awarded the book prize. During this year there were many visits paid to the school by Ministry of Education officials who were working on developing the new Zimbabwe teaching curriculum including the use of locally produced Zimbabwean textbooks and the requirement to sit Grade 7 examinations as a prerequisite to entering Form 1. We were also required to take ChiShona, and surprisingly, our first teacher was a white man. I also began to participate more in sports and was selected for the tennis team. I thoroughly enjoyed the numerous field trips to sites of interest including granite outcrops, the museum and the airport. We had to write up our findings in projects and/or paint what we had seen. I was awarded a second place certificate in 30m freestyle at our annual gala. We used to have extra mural activities including science with the headmaster Mr. Cracknell. There was a constant popularity contest amongst boys and Karl van Dyke earned this position rather rapidly given his handsome blonde looks and his flashy gold watch. Nikki Opie was his girlfriend. We used to have end-of-term parties that ran way into the night. I have kept in contact with some of my class mates including Sheona Kaschula who now lives in Australia. Another popular boy was Brian Townsend and I was to meet him again 17 years later after we parted ways at Avondale.

I looked forward to my final year in Grade 7M in 1982 as it was with a humorous teacher, Mr. Hay. I had know of him mainly from his clowning antiques, chasing children around the school field, mud bathing students during cross country, operating the cinema camera and throwing large Christmas parties with his characteristic chicken dance manoeuvres. He had quite a temper though and used to beat students with a plank. He characteristically always used to drink a bottle of coke. He made us participate in gardening and we were all requested to collect dried manure with our bare hands. The idea was to sell vegetables to make money for the school. During this year two former pupils broke into the caretaker's office and used the keys to open the classrooms and hall where they caused tens of thousands of dollars in damage by squirting paint into the piano, ribboning the stage curtains, smashing furniture and personal items in classrooms and spreading fresh plaster-of-paris all over the art room floor. The CID quickly apprehended the culprits who were cordially sentenced to seven years in Kadoma (then Gatooma) Juvenile Detention Centre. They opened my desk but did not damage the contents. They did, however, pour a bottle of tomato sauce and Indian ink all over Mr. Hay's desk.

I did remarkably well in Science and Mr. Hay noted, "A very good standard of work from Ross in all the content subjects. His written work is very good and his illustrations excellent". My final year report in December 1982 had the general remarks, "Ross has worked very well this year and has attained a high standard of work. He's been a pleasant pupil although a little too much on the quiet and reserved side. Ross attained first position in class". This was followed by a comment from the Headmaster, "Very pleasing progress. Best wishes for the future." So ended my life in Primary School. Interestingly, 1982 was the first time I attempted to draw my first unpublished cartoon book, entitled, "Battle of the Sky!".

Preparation for high school was rather daunting and there were lots of welcome packs to read through. Vainona High School was one of the best achieving high schools in the country both academically and extra-murally. Its motto was, "Bene Mereamur de Patribus", translated let us deserve well of our forefathers. The school clubs Heany, Borrow and Johnson were named after the British South African Company (BSAC) pioneers on whose land the school was built. Historically Johnson met Cecil John Rhodes in 1889 and was awarded the contract to organise, equip and lead the Pioneer Corps to occupy Mashonaland, build a road between Palapye and Mount Hampden (Fort Salisbury) and begin construction of settlements along the route fit for civil government with protection provided by the BSAC's Police (BSAP). After fulfilling his contract and the disbandment of the Pioneer Corps, Johnson, together with Heany and Borrow, became actively engaged in land and mining development in Mashonaland. Rhodes himself later invested in the Company to strengthen its capital structure as Johnson's profits from organizing the Pioneer Corps were inadequate for contemplated mining development.

I remember sitting on the floor of the school hall on the first day of my enrolment at Vainona High and the Headmaster Mr. P.J. Snyder gave us a welcome speech followed by a roll call to our respective classes. We were all given a very hard time as we were required to pass a Form One Prefects test on facts about the school and its background. Painstakingly we had to memorise all the Prefect's names and were bullied into the ground, often being forced to do errands for the Sixth Formers. I believe it was a way of re-enforcing the concept of respect for one's elders, although it was taken to extremes at times. One bully, Ian Broom, was notorious for punching one on the arm and hand-cuffing Form Ones to the rugby horse. We were forced to attend and support the first teams in our school, especially the rugby team. We were also required to participate in sports and cultural events. We were subjected to a very strict attire requirement – haircut, uniform, garter, shoe and hymnbook checks. If we failed any of these we were beaten, usually by the deputy head, humorously describing it as two lashes. Other punishments included manual labour on a Friday afternoon that involved slashing grass, scrubbing floors, collecting litter and/or lifting items in the school hall. I was once chucked on manual labour for not opening my mouth loud enough during recital of the school anthem! Manual labour lists used to be read out by the head boy or girl during Friday morning assembly. Reflecting, this system was ridiculously autocratic and unnecessary, and instilled fear in pupils instead of building confidence. It was, though, a means of discipline.

I had to start school at 0730 hr and the latest we were allowed in the school gate was 0725 hr otherwise our name would be taken. Persistent latecomers were expelled. I therefore had to get up at 0600 hr to walk or cycle to school in time. Sports and clubs were compulsory and following this we would have to complete homework and study for class tests and examinations. It was a full house until the school holiday and there was little time to relax, as we usually had sports events on Saturday either as the host school or as a visiting team to another school. Competition amongst sports matches and in class examinations was very stiff indeed, and it was a real confidence booster when I did well. We were awarded with book prizes for achieving first or second position in class and colours for sporting or club achievements. Service shields and cups were won for achievements, the victor ludorum cup for the best overall sports person. Academic achievements were noted for seven or more A-grades at O-Level and two or more A-grades at A-Level. In 1983, students could also sit M-Level and S-Level examinations. Form Two's had to sit an obligatory Zimbabwean Junior Certificate (ZJC) examination and Form Three's a National Examination Council (NEC) examination. The latter was subsequently dropped from the teaching curricula in 1984. In many ways the Government schools gave a better level of all-round education than the private schools. In the early 1980s, Vainona High School was regarded as one of the best Government schools in the country as one student, Morgan Warner, had country-wide attained the most A grades at O-Level .

In my first term's report in 1983, I was aged 13 years and 2 months, the form average age being 14 years and 1 month. The comments from teachers on ten subjects were mostly complimentary, although the comments received for games and clubs were quite critical. The headmaster, Mr. Snyder, however commented that I had had a good first term at High School. It was following the Form One grading tests that I was placed into the A2 stream in the second term in which I achieved first place in the class examinations and was awarded the class prize. Thereafter I entered the A1 stream in the third term. I tried very hard in the new class and did very well in Geography, Afrikaans, Shona and History. As a consequence I achieved eighth position in class.

Registration was followed shortly afterwards by assembly, a formal event during which we had to line up outside the hall and enter by way of seniority. Sixth formers were always permitted to enter and leave first. I do remember one occasion, however, when the head boy was dissatisfied with the sixth form conduct and they were made to sit in the front of the hall in the place of the Form Ones. During assembly there would be an opening prayer followed by the headmaster announcements and a hymn. Sports and club teams were usually read out by the headmaster, as were results of matches played. We had to stand when the headmaster or an appointee walked in and mounted the stage. Staff members sat on chairs behind the headmaster's lectern. Once all staff had left the head girl made her announcements followed by the head boy. Usually there was a roll call for manual labour announced by surname and form. At irregular intervals we were surprised by a dress, haircut, garter or hymn book check. Failure thereof was punished with manual labour for girls and beats for boys. There was no leniency and the only excuse for failing to attend a sports or club practice was a sick note. Punishment was also exacted for failure to complete homework and talking in class.

I was an active participant in debating, chess, table tennis and science clubs. Debating was extremely interesting especially when we travelled to other schools like Peterhouse in Marondera (formerly Marandellas) which offered us numerous scones and cakes afterwards. Trips to the Catholic run schools like the Convent, Saint Georges and Saint Ignatius were also interesting from the perspective that the teachers were nuns and priests. We were of course expected to wear our full formal uniform which included a white long-sleeved shirt and tie, blazer and grey trousers. For each club we had to attend once-a-week sessions where we practiced our skills. Although table tennis and science clubs were fun, there tended to be a certain degree of bullying from the older forms and we were granted only minimum practice time. Science club prepared us for open days and we were all assigned an experiment to complete. I was asked to carry out a combustion and glass blowing experiment. I remember the brilliant flame produced from burning magnesium. We interacted with schools within the vicinity of the Harare area. Some sporting events, however, took students to the far recesses of the country where they had to stay overnight at the school. As you can imagine, this would prove disruptive to one's homework, and thankfully this never happened to me.

Whilst at high school I kept numerous pets at home including mice, rats and guinea pigs. My brother and I took it in turns to clean their cages and feed them. We used to sell the litters to pet shops. The rat and mouse food was a mixture of Pronutro® porridge and vegetable scraps. What I think was very interesting was constructing their cages and feeding them a variety of insects. We used to spend many hours playing with the animals keeping a weary look out for dogs and cats lest they kill them. I also indulged in vegetable cultivation referring to the classic Tom Manson's garden book which had a useful monthly cultivation of vegetables. I attempted to look after the fruit trees without much success. The banana plantation produced many bunches which were either eaten fresh or sun dried. The avocado pear tree did not produce any fruit, but once a nail had been driven into its trunk, we were showered with copious avocados. The dogs often used to eat them.

Present, Jason's three-legged dog, used to sleep on his blanket on the kitchen floor. We fed him dog meal porridge boiled up with pet meat and bones. He used to love his walks and would recognise the tinkering of the dog lead. He was a loyal dog and he often caught small rodents and brought them to us as presents. It was unfortunate that he developed extensive cancer aged 10 years eight months and given the pain he was in, it was decided to put him down. We buried him wrapped in his blanket.

His replacement Henry, a mongrel, was rescued from an abusive owner. He was very frivolous as a puppy and used to chase the cats wildly around the yard. He disliked the gardener especially when he approached the house each morning. If we were in need of a watch dog, we certainly had one in Henry. A major problem in Zimbabwe was the constant break-ins and nearly everybody had a guard dog of some sort. Henry saved us from loss on many an occasion.

Ross Cooper and Henry, Harare, 1990

Jason Cooper with Henry on Vainona High School sports field, Harare, 1991

Jason Cooper celebrating at his Grandparents 50th Wedding Anniversary, Harare, 1990

**A new Labrador cross puppy replaced the late Henry,
Vainona, Harare**

Form Two in Zimbabwe was a year to be taken seriously as it was the first public examination at secondary school, the Zimbabwe Junior Certificate of Education (ZJC). I studied for seven taught subjects and one un-taught subject, Religious Education, which I prepared for on my own. Again, as before, each term compulsorily required us to take up two sports and a club. I remember doing very well, my best, in the third term assessments with seven honours.

O-Levels required a great deal of study and following our mock examination results we had to practice many a past-paper to excel. Many of our teachers were expatriate and pretty keen to help us achieve top grades. The situation in England was hard at the time with little prospects of teaching work. Hence they came in droves to teach in Zimbabwe. In the end, I attained six As and four Bs in the Cambridge set-examinations. A-Level registration was tedious as we had to each individually meet with the headmaster to discuss the subjects we would like to take. We were each forced to take the

General Paper in addition to three or four A-Level subjects. The teachers were not good and one was left to do most of the work on one's own. We also had a shortage of textbooks and ended up sharing. What was particularly difficult were the practicals. We had to do five dissections in addition to a practical paper and three theory papers for A-Level Biology. Chemistry had four papers, Mathematics two. I never remembered an afternoon without studying. In the Sixth Form we also had to participate in sports, athletics and clubs. I achieved a good testimonial at the end and was glad to put my school days behind me and enter university. I also made plans to leave home and rent a room, becoming independent. My first place was a caravan which I occupied for five months in a garden close to Harare's railway shunting yard. I once placed two one cent coins on the railway track and came back later to find them flattened as thin as paper!

Pamuzinda Safari Lodge

Located along the Bulawayo Road in Harare, Zimbabwe is a safari lodge situated on the banks of the Seruwi River in the middle of a private 5,000-acre game park. Images used were obtained with the permission of Mrs. C. Jessup who visited the Lodge in 1990.

Elephants!

Giraffe!

Solitary rhinoceros and a baobab tree

Rhinoceros and Sable Antelope

6

LIFE AS A STUDENT AND EMPLOYEE AT THE UNIVERSITY OF ZIMBABWE (1990 – 1993, 1995 – 2001, 2003)

A first year university student is always excited at the prospect of entering an institute of higher education for the first time, and once the daunting registration process is complete, begins to enjoy himself, at least for the first week. The work load though quickly sets in and suddenly one is faced with sleepless nights and trekking from one lecture hall to another, a whole day's work of theory and practicals. In fact when I was at the Mount Pleasant campus at the University of Zimbabwe (UZ) I rarely had any chance to enjoy myself. Lectures would commence at 0800 hr and no late comers would be permitted to enter. This meant that I had to get up at 0600 hr and after having breakfast, jump onto my bicycle and cycle to the lecture hall. Lectures were principally didactic with the lecturer presenting hand-written notes either on an overhead projector or on a chalk board. One quickly had to learn how to manage one's time as the workload was excessive. Tests were either multiple-choice with negative marking or essay-type. Every single practical session had to be written up. Markers were perceived as being overly strict. It was interesting to note the vast variety of expatriate lecturers, Zimbabwe drawing them due to its economic prosperity. We did, however, find it hard to understand the Bulgarian lecturers as their pronunciation verged on the exotic.

Ross Cooper on his bicycle, Vainona, Harare

Ross Cooper in a suit!

Although I faired pretty well in the assignments and some of the tests, I did not perform very well in the examinations. I found the content hard going especially from the rapid spewing out of information during a session and thereafter to go away and write notes on the topic. It did assist one to buy second-hand textbooks from previous students but it took a lot of stamina to remember all the information. We were also sent on field trips, some of which commenced on a Saturday.

The food was nice at the campus and very affordable. I remember paying $2.00 for tea-bone steak and chips. I often had buns, doughnuts and coffee at 1000 hr, before commencement of lectures at 1100 hr. The dining hall in the students' union was massive and it was nice to sit in an area that overlooked the swimming pool. Indeed, the university grounds were most impressive with easy access to pubic transport and the Emergency Taxi (ET) into the city centre. Located on a hill, the university was once a granite quarry through which a railway line passed. Ideally, unlike many European universities, all Faculties were located on one site with both staff and student accommodation. The grounds also encompassed a wild vlei area with a river, providing ample opportunity for research projects. The campus, located on a hill, was surrounded by Mount Pleasant High School and the Ministry of Education, School Examination Council Offices and main roads. A former teacher's hostel used as student accommodation, was converted into administrative and IT offices, and the dining hall into a privately-run catering facility. I frequented this dining hall principally during my lecturing years right up until 2003. I used to collect all the meat bones and sadza (maize meal) left-overs and take them home for our dogs.

My first graduation was one of the best days of my life and I was very happy to celebrate the completion of an extremely difficult degree programme. I was happy that my family and friends could attend the ceremony to celebrate the special day.

As ever one wonders about the romances of university students. I, however, never indulged and stuck to friends, many of whom were church-goers. I did have a pen-girlfriend though.

On campus we used to meet up in residences and share notes and textbooks. I remember Menfree Tanyanyiwa who used to bring me food from the student canteen in the student complexes.

**Ross Cooper as an undergraduate student,
University of Zimbabwe, 1992**

The food was so abundant that students used to have food fights and, of course, there was a lot of wastage. Generally blacks, whites and Indians got along, although there was the occasional, disturbing talk of politics usually fuelled by Mugabe. When students dared to demonstrate they were brutally crushed by Mugabe's riot police using tear gas, rubber batons, and later, live ammunition. Many of these riots were, however, unnecessary given the provision of student loans and the vast supply of American-donated textbooks, journals and practical facilities, and severely disrupted our studies. Student union leaders would boycott lectures without the consent of the entire student population, resulting in lost lessons and us entering the examination halls unprepared. It was hard to attain a first-class as this was pegged at 85% plus. In order for one to progress from a Bachelor's degree to a Master's, M.Phil. or D.Phil. degree, one had to attain at least a 2.1 classification. I always aspired to complete a D.Phil. degree and was fortunate to obtain a 2.1 honour classification.

Ross Cooper's first graduation, Harare Botanical Gardens, 1994

Happy celebrations!

**Menfree Tanyanyiwa and Ross Cooper watching
a UZ basketball match**

After leaving university I worked as a science and Biology teacher for a while and then returned to begin registration as an M.Phil. student in the Faculty of Medicine. Unfortunately my first proposal on the chronic effects of chloroquine on embryonic development was rejected and I had to begin from scratch again. The hard thing about an M.Phil. degree was that we, the students, had to compose, present and defend it. Supervisors were distant and this dissuaded many an applicant from continuing. I, however, refused to give up and successfully presented a proposal on the effects of concurrent intake of chloroquine and ethanol on renal function in the male Sprague-Dawley rat. The surgery of the rats was very hard, tedious and took many hours of practice to master. Often they would die under anaesthesia. If a rat was successfully prepared it may not produce sufficient quantities of urine, or upon analysis, the electrolyte concentrations would be deviant. It took a lot of learning on my part and dodged determination. My supervisor mostly left me to my own devices and this meant that I had to find new ways of coping and completing the work. I was fortunate to secure demonstrator and research assistant positions which provided a salary to help me pay my rent and buy food.

Another award! Ross Cooper and his Grandfather outside
Harare Sheraton Hotel, Harare, 1997

Zimbabweans of all races waiting to graduate!

The role of an M.Phil. student was very subjective and the Victorian style of instruction left one thinking if it was actually worth continuing with the studies, especially in light of the many experimental failures, some of which included those induced by electricity cuts and others by shortages of chemical and equipment. However, we Zimbabweans were always ready to make a plan and found solutions. It was important that one published papers and attended conferences. I was, however disappointed that my supervisor was usually first author on my publications and that I never got the chance to go on any external conferences. I resigned my position in 2001 given the collapse of the Zimbabwean economy and flew to the UK.

Ross Cooper (right) and Professor Graham Hill (left, front table) (UZ Vice Chancellor) in the Great Hall, University of Zimbabwe, Harare

Department of Physiology, University of Zimbabwe

Ross Cooper watching the total eclipse of the sun, Harare, 2001

A happy day in Bulawayo in my father's garden

In 2003, however, I returned to Zimbabwe elated and pleased to be back in my country, where I took up immediate employment at the University of Zimbabwe. UK had been very taxing on my resolve and I was tired of working short-term contracts. However, I was soon to learn the extent of the economic collapse, and perhaps, I dwelt too much on that. I should have gone out more and interacted with my peers. Jason, visiting Harare in 2003, encouraged me to do this. A continued stay in Harare seemed untenable though, and towards the end of the year I was offered a short-term contract in Bristol University with the flight included. I decided, rightly or wrongly, to take up the offer, with the hope of returning to Zimbabwe once the contract had finished. I was, fortunate, though, in late 2003, to be offered a permanent senior lectureship in Birmingham and made plans to settle there.

Happily fishing in Nyanga

Ross Cooper tubing in Nyanga

World's View, Nyanga, Zimbabwe

Pomona Farm, Harare

Street in Vainona, Harare

7

A DARK CLOUD DESCENDS (FINANCIAL, ECONOMIC AND PRODUCTIVE DEMISE)

In 1999, the situation in Zimbabwe drastically deteriorated once the national referendum of a no vote was reached for Mugabe not to extend his presidency. Like many dictators before him, Mugabe chose scapegoats for his crimes and unleashed a reign of terror and destruction on the white farming community, escalating in 2000, much of which has continued unabated. A mineral- and agriculturally-rich country should have been independent of the West long ago, yet Mugabe chose to stir up popular feeling against the hard-working white farming community by demanding their land back without any compensation for distribution to landless blacks.

**Worry is clearly evident on the faces of the family
of harassed white farmers**

**Repossessed farm along the Bulawayo Road lying unused
and over-grown**

Instead it was a rampant land-grab and ministers and officials and their families were the principal beneficiaries. Some animals were more equal than others as depicted in George Orwell's Animal Farm. The Mugabe-orchestrated farm invasions were catastrophic and plunged the country into economic chaos. Instead of the people mustering the courage and resources to appose the Mugabe regime, many fled the country in droves abandoning careers, lives and properties. The collapse of the health sector and teaching and universities followed in quick succession as staff left, usually without notice, to seek greener pastures abroad. People often say that the last kick of a dying horse is the deadliest and things will get better. Clearly, though, the Zanu-PF machinery would have to go, before any positive change could occur. Described by many as the butcher of Harare, Mugabe was bent on seeing the loss of life and the breaking down every facet of Zimbabwean society. The constant media highlight of Zimbabwe and the dreadful consequences of his appalling leadership with the onset of pandemic cholera and increase in anthrax cases in 2008, created a feeling of absolute and dire helplessness. Additionally, for many Zimbabweans, life abroad has been hard and homesickness abounds.

At independence, Harare was a sprawling megalopolis consisting of 128 suburbs (Appendix 1) and there was the issuance of new $2, 5, 10 and $20 bank notes (Appendix 2) to replace the $1, 2 and 10 Rhodesian notes issued by the Reserve Bank of Rhodesia in 1970, and the $5 in 1972 (Appendix 3). In 1970, the bronze ½ and 1 cent and the cupro-nickel 2½ cent coins were introduced. New 5 cent coins were introduced in 1973 followed by 10, 20 and 25 cents in 1975. All coins were issued up until 1977. In 1981 the Rhodesian dollar was demonetised under Statutory Instrument 378 of the Government of Zimbabwe. The Zimbabwean dollar was introduced as a coin in 1980 and was worth more than the US $ (1 ZWD = 1.47 USD). Economic mismanagement, however, saw the drastic erosion of its value such that by 26th July 2006, the parallel market value of the Zimbabwean dollar fell to one million to the British pound. The saga continued unabated and on 16th January 2009 it was announced by the Reserve Bank of Zimbabwe that they would be printing a $100 trillion note together with new $50, 20 and 10 trillion notes. Incredibly a loaf of bread cost $300 billion and the price of all commodities increased daily. The official rate of inflation reached 231 million percent in July 2007. Shop sellers preferred to be paid in foreign currency which included the US dollar, South African rand or the Botswana pula. The collapse of the public service sector has seen doctors and nurses off work since September 2007 as their wages were not being paid in US dollars. The strike has coincided with a devastating cholera epidemic which has claimed over 2000 lives. Teachers have also left their jobs in droves delaying the opening of schools and the release of examination results.

The Zanu-PF government allows its members to obtain foreign currency at the official bank exchange rate and this equates to nothing as the real inflation rate would mean that on their wages they would get very little indeed. Their lavish lifestyles and Mercedes Benz cars are shocking as most people in Europe cannot afford to run such vehicles. It suits the Zanu-PF politburo for Mugabe to stay in power so that they can cream as much money as they like out of the system.

In 1980 coins were introduced as 1, 5, 10, 20, 50 cents and 1 dollar. The 1 cent was minted in bronze and the remainder in cupro-nickel. Bronze-plated steel replaced bronze in 1989 and a 2 dollar coin was introduced in 1997. In 2001, nickel-plated steel replaced cupro-nickel in the 10, 20 and 50 cents and 1 dollar, and a bimetallic 5 dollar coin was introduced. Although plans for the minting of new $5,000 and $10,000 were announced in June 2005, the coins failed to appear on the market. All old coinage was re-introduced at face value to the third dollar in August 2008 and new $10 and $25 coins were circulated having been minted in 2003 but only issued with the redenomination.

The second Zimbabwe dollar was discussed for due issuance in October 2005 by the Reserve Bank of Zimbabwe although in June 2006 the Deputy Finance Minister stated that only on the achievement of macro-economic stability (double-digit inflation) would the new currency be introduced. The dollar was redenominated in August 2006 at a rate of one devalued dollar being equivalent to 1000 old dollars. The typical blame- the-Zimbabwean-public syndrome saw in March-June 2007 the outlawing of any price increase on commodities. The Reserve Bank in the meantime was stock-piling the bank notes. Then the bank announced that it would cut off three zeros from the dollar whence one dollar would be one million of the old dollars. Absolute pandemonium and chaos reigned in the commercial and industrial spheres. The 6th September 2007 saw a further devaluation of the dollar by 92% with an official exchange rate of ZW$30,000: US$1, although the black market rate was ZW$600,000: US$1.

The third dollar announcement in July 2008 was that ZW$10 billion would be equivalent to ZW$1. At the time the planned denominations issued were coins valued at ZW$5, 10 and 25 and banknotes worth ZW$5, 10, 20, 100 and 500. However, due to the frequent cash shortages and the worthless Zimbabwean dollar, foreign currency was legalized as a de facto currency on 13th September 2008. The ever rising inflation however meant that the Reserve Bank had to continually print notes resulting in ten zeros appearing at the end of 2008. A bank note of ZW$100 billion could only pay for three eggs, a dramatic example of hyperinflation (Appendix 4).

Hyperinflation reached 623% in January 2004 and fell back to low triple digits in 2004 thereafter surging to 1,282.1% in 2006. In April 2007 inflation reached 3,714% with the monthly rate for April exceeding 100% and a sustained rate over 12 months was predicted to result in an annual inflation of over 400,000%. Mid-year inflation in 2007 was 4,530%. The ineptitude and callousness of the government was shown by their refusal to publish inflation figures, a deliberate steer away from the unprecedented hyperinflation. In July 2007 the Consumer Council of Zimbabwe (CCZ) announced that inflation was exceeding 13,000%. The Central Statistics Office (CSO) last reported in February 2007 an annual inflation of 1,729%. In September 2007 the CSO announced an official inflation rate of 6,592.8% in August 2007, although private estimates were as high as 20,000%. By November 2007 they announced an official inflation rate of 14,840.5% for October 2007. The problem with the rapidly rising inflation was that the computers could not cope with the excessive zeros. In February 2008 the CSO announced an inflation rate for December 2007 at 66,212.3% and unofficially at Z$7.1 million to the US$. In February 2008 the CSO announced that inflation had reached 100,580.2%, and in April it reached 164,900.3%. In May 2008 it reached 355,000%. An independent financial assessment, however, predicted that in May 2008 inflation reached 1,063,572.6%. In June 2008 the CSO said that the inflation had risen from 7,336,000% to 9,030,000%, being set at 10,500,000% by the end of the month. Other, possibly more reliable sources, reported that inflation was likely to be two million percent in May 2008 and, according to Zimbabwean economist John Robertson, 10-15 million percent in June 2008. Robertson estimated that inflation was 40-50 million percent in July 2008, and the CSO stated that inflation rose to 231 million percent in July 2008.

In February 2006 the Reserve Bank stated that the government had printed ZW$20.5 trillion in order to buy foreign currency to pay off the IMF debt. This was followed by another announcement that in May 2006, the government would procure another ZW$60 trillion, much of which was diverted for use to pay the 300% increase in wages of soldiers and policemen and the 200% increase for civil servants. There were many problems, however, as the government failed to secure forex to pay for ink and paper.

One has to realise that the bearer's cheque has an expiry date and in August 2006, approximately ZW$10 trillion old dollars had not been exchanged for revalued dollars and were demonetized. The direct involvement of Mugabe in the financial mess was justified when he ordered the Reserve Bank governor to print an additional ZW$1 trillion to cover the civil servants' and soldiers' salaries hiked by 600 and 900%, respectively. In July 2007 Mugabe said money would be continuously printed to fund municipal projects. In August 2007 there was an additional ZW$3 trillion printed to pay for 500,000 scotch carts and 800,000 ox-drawn ploughs plus cattle. Whether the money was actually used for this is highly questionable. Underpaid people engaged in black market forex trading to supplement their income. In November 2007 it was reported that the money supply was ZW$58 trillion revalued money of which ZW$56-7 trillion was being held by the public. In January 2008 the money supply had increased by ZW$33 trillion and the demonetization of ZW$200,000 bearer cheques was put on hold in order to increase the money supply. In January 2008 the Reserve Bank reported that the money supply had been increased to ZW$170 trillion since December. The Munich Company Giesecke and Devriet was being paid £382,000/week to deliver bank notes at ZW$170 trillion/week. However, in July 2008 the German company stopped printing notes after pressure from the German government. This was followed by an Austro-Hungarian company who supplied to the Reserve bank the licenses and software to design and print Zimbabwean currency. Massive cash withdrawal limits were imposed by the regime and the Institute of Commercial Management reported that £1 = ZW$1.2 trillion.

In April 2009, having adopted the South African Rand (ZAR) and the United States Dollar (US$) as legal tender, shops became filled with food, utensils, clothes and other commodities. The average man on the street, however, complained that although things were better, the lack of insufficient funds meant that there was not enough to buy sufficient food. The street exchange rate of 9 ZAR: 1 US$ in the shops meant that the value of US$ spending went further, although the public were weary of spending the like due to the lack of change in shops. Another worry was the influx of forged US$ notes.

Mugabe accused the entire white farming community of not being forthcoming and willing to give up their land. This of course was wrong as a fair deal would have required that they be compensated and the right of choice as to whether they wanted to relinquish their land or not. Numerous farmers in fact did offer parts of their land and unused farms to the government. In 2000, Mugabe provided army trucks to ferry gangs of unemployed youths to harass and kill farmers. The Daily News, whose press was later land-mine blown-up on the orders of Mugabe, reported severe beatings, rapes, killings and abductions. In all 14 white farmers and countless numbers of black workers lost their lives. Children were caught in the cross-fire. Friends in Concession, a crop-growing region just beyond the Mazowe district, described how they were given just 24 hours to get off their farm. Many farmers called the police, who blatantly ignored their pleas clearly on the orders of government. The carnage was spearheaded by Border Gezi and Chenjerai Hitler Hunzvi, a medical doctor who was guilty of crimes against humanity. They were both later to die, Gezi in a mysterious car accident and Hunzvi from AIDS. Mugabe is prepared to allow the elimination of rivals when they threaten his power.

Such actions were clearly very damaging to the economy of Zimbabwe and resulted in an exodus of white farmers, many of whom have been gratefully received by other African countries including Nigeria, Ghana, Uganda, Kenya, Zambia, Mozambique, Botswana and Namibia. The West was quick to condemn the violence and wanton destruction but has, until now, done nothing substantiative except impose travel bans and freeze accounts of black-listed members of the Zanu-PF faction. The cruelty of Zanu-PF militia is evidenced in their readiness to use pliers to tear the lips off Movement for Democratic Change (MDC) supporters, inflicting beatings with iron bars, gang raping and shooting people, usually in the presence of their children. The Zimbabwean people have been so badly abused, weakened and divided that it is unlikely they will ever be able to muster any strength to form a collective military force or other to over-throw Mugabe. The unbending support of Zimbabwe by South Africa has been a big player in the regime's success. One would ask if is it really tribal and anti-colonial support, or, instead, the fact that it suits neighbouring countries to see Zimbabwe fail as it provides increased global trade for them. Unless Africa is prepared to help itself, eliminate greed and corruption, and to recognise that if managed properly, one's country would be economically very powerful, there is little hope that the state of its nations will improve. The once beautiful and iridescent flame lily has withered. It is a prolonged drought and the soil is parched. The dust is blowing away. The roots are exposed. No nutrients. The death of a plant! The death of a bread-basket country!

8

MOVE TO ENGLAND

Although graduation day was exciting and the fact that I was the only D.Phil. grandaunt in the Faculty of Medicine, it signalled the end of my career at the University of Zimbabwe and my move to UK. It was not easy to leave Zimbabwe. I looked forward to seeing my brother again after a three year absence. The writing was on the wall for Zimbabwe and the unbending and utterly ruthless actions of the butcher of Harare created despair in people's hearts. Mugabe had steadily ruined Zimbabwe and although there was a drive to educate the masses, there were no jobs to absorb them. The rapidly declining monetary value of the dollar meant that we academics were attracted like iron-to-magnet to seek employment abroad. The University of Zimbabwe is now barely functional, stripped of most of its equipment and resources, and mostly closed. Other functional units including health care, schooling and commerce have also been rapidly deteriorating. The Avenues Clinic, a privately-funded hospital, now requires one to deposit US$2,000 before admittance. Mugabe's actions have resulted in the direct and indirect deaths of countless thousands of innocent people.

Proud D.Phil. graduate, 2001

Climbing aboard the Ethiopian Airways flight to London in the early hours of the morning was exciting and as we took off the sun-rays streamed through the jet. The flight had many stops though – Nairobi, Addis Ababa and Athens. As a consequence the flight was 4 hours late touching down at Heathrow, London. On arrival I was met by Jason and two friends, who promptly took me onto the tube. Although we were all smiles, everybody on the tube looked miserable, cold and distant. I was soon to learn how hard it was to survive in the UK. Having missed the last train to Leicester, we had to spend the night in London at our step-sister Fern's rented house. This gave us a chance to catch up on old times. The Sunday morning trip back to King's Cross was better as it was less crowded and soon we were on a fast train to Leicester. I remember looking at the greenery of the countryside. I wondered if I had made the right choice coming to UK and, being exhausted, missed my bed in Harare. It was cold and windy. How long would I take to get used to it, I wondered.

Fortunately my brother had organised via his landlord friend Jethro Swift for me to stay temporarily in his house until I found my feet. I started off sleeping on a mattress on the lounge floor. I had a lot to sort out including getting a bank account opened and registering on the National Social Security register to obtain my National Insurance number. Registering with work agencies was tiresome due to the multitude of forms and requirements thereof. They always needed relevant references which made things difficult as my latest references were in Zimbabwe. I managed, however, to find some menial work and settled down into a council bottle collection job. Thereafter I made my way to Poland to do some research work at the Institute of Genetics and Animal Breeding. At the time Poland was not a member of the EU and the equipment in the laboratories was very outdated. However, the people were very welcoming and I thoroughly enjoyed my short stay over there. I regretted not taking up an offer of teaching post-graduate students English, at the time, deeming the pay too low. I have, however, maintained an extremely good collaboration with the institute and have been invited numerous times to attend and engage in research. The institute has successfully obtained EU funding for continuance of genetic research into animal breeds and lines.

9

ACADEMIC LIFE IN ENGLAND

Ross Cooper in Hampstead Heath, London, 2003

I was very grateful for the generosity shown to me by Judy Harris at Bristol University in agreeing to pay for my flight and shipping in advance of my taking up employment on a fixed term contract teaching Physiology to first and second year students. On arrival in Bristol I was given a room in Manor Hall and quickly began planning my role both as a research associate and Physiology laboratory demonstrator. I also engaged in part-time supply teaching to supplement my income. I was fortunate enough to gain a place as a hall tutor in block A-B of Churchill Hall. I fixed up two old discarded bicycles and cycled into work everyday including during snow storms. The one down-side to the halls was the noise, the drunken parties and the setting off of fire-alarms. My sleep suffered. I also felt somewhat insecure as I had no future job prospect once my contract had expired, so I was pleased to be offered the same year, a senior lectureship in Birmingham.

Bristol was very picturesque especially on the Downs and the view of the suspension bridge. I liked the academic interaction and helpfulness of the staff. Security was, however, excessive, requiring us to use swipe cards and I remember there being a host of door codes. The bicycle shed also had a swipe-card system and required us to lock them securely.

Student education was very intense, hands-on and tutorial-based. This method of teaching was vastly different from that in the University of Zimbabwe which expected the student to do most of the work. Therefore, I had to adapt quickly and the helpful support from Eugene Lloyd made things much more enjoyable. Bristol Medical School was in 2004 rated number three in the UK and, as such, standards were high. I was slightly disappointed, though, that we weren't able to engage in any research work.

I rented a double room in a shared house and cycled into work. Despite the traffic, the ride was pleasant and took me about 40 minutes. I quickly embarked on lecturing large groups of students. There was an expectation that one should just get on with the tasks, requiring one's thoughtful initiative.

Snow at Churchill Hall, Bristol

I generally found the brumie students to be keen learners and engaged in their tasks wholeheartedly. A lot of time was taken up preparing and delivering sessions on Anatomy and Physiology. Time permitting, there was the opportunity to engage in research. Surprisingly I noticed that a fair proportion of the classes comprised Zimbabwean nursing students.

One of the greatest benefits of working abroad was the opportunity to attend conferences, something that was very limited in Africa due to lack of sufficient funding. An external sponsor could be approached to fund the costs, but this was extremely competitive. Some of my most enjoyable trips included those to Brazil, Latvia, Poland and Australia.

Ross Cooper in Egypt, 2006

Ross Cooper in Sutton Park, Sutton Coldfield, Birmingham

Canadian Geese enjoying canal life, Fazely Canal, Birmingham

Geese walking on top of a frozen canal, Fazely Canal, Birmingham

Plants-Brook Reservoirs, Pype Hayes, Birmingham

10

THE NIGHT IS DARKEST BEFORE DAWN

Despite the depravity in Zimbabwe, many of its citizens living abroad feel that one day they will return home. This seems ludicrous given that many of them had initially voted for Mugabe and are unwilling and incapable of taking up arms. Brave faces appearing every weekend to demonstrate outside the Zimbabwe embassy in London, are ignored. Who is going to help? In reality, nobody but the people of Zimbabwe! Mugabe's advanced age may be on the side of Zimbabwe though. Many believe that once he is gone, things will begin to improve. It's hard to ignore the fact that masses of Zanu-PF thugs may be fighting for a seat in power once Mugabe goes, though, and clearly a total purge of their curse will have to be fulfilled. A country can never exist in isolation, separated from the rest of the world.

The year 2008 was possibly the worst year so far for Zimbabwe with the hyperinflation reaching unprecedented heights, a deliberate action by Mugabe to keep the regime alive. The end of the year and the beginning of 2009 has seen a record number of cholera deaths. On the 13th January 2009, fresh data released by the World Health Organisation showed that the total cholera deaths had amounted to 2,024 with a total infected population of 39,806. As Prime Minister Gordon Brown of Britain put it –Mugabe and his Zanu-PF government clearly have no concern whatsoever for the well-being of the citizens of Zimbabwe. The abduction and exclusion of MDC activists, and the deliberate stalling of talks by Mugabe for a power-sharing agreement, has resulted in an ever deepening crisis. The attempts by Gordon Brown to try and convince the UN Security Council to act against Zimbabwe have been in vain, because tallied council votes of agreement are more important than innocent lives. Corrupt firms dealing in arms and printing propaganda leaflets have made a lot of money out of the Zimbabwean plight. Worse of all is that people are dying of starvation. Rural folk have been reduced to eating wild fruits, berries and animals. The rare and endangered animal species are also threatened. Nearly all wildlife sanctuaries and the breeding populations of white and black rhinoceros have been obliterated. The national cattle herd is also virtually annihilated, breeds of which took many decades to sire. They were selectively bred to resist parasitic diseases and drought. The piles of uncollected garbage in cities have resulted in the emergence of large vermin populations. The risk of the bubonic plague is real.

The question of many authors is what will happen after Mugabe has left power? Will the professionals and farmers who have left Zimbabwe be willing to return? The gap in the current generation will have lasting consequences for decades within the socio-economic arena. Many that do return will learn of the deaths of family, friends and relations. It will certainly take a Herculean effort on behalf of the surviving Zimbabwean diasporas supported by the full co-operation of the international community many years before any semblance of high standards will be forthcoming. Mugabe has not helped the reputation of Africa, a continent fraught with bad governance and leadership. The injustices of colonialism perpetrated by the BSAC in the 1890s cannot be denied. Mugabe claims that he has single hand:ily liberated Zimbabwe from colonialism. In reality, though, his bad governance has utterly ruined it. What darkness exists in the depth of his soul and his childhood? Never in the history of Zimbabwe has its people seen somebody so unbending and cruel. May he be the last! May our national flower the flame lily once more blossom and extend its tentacled vines through the undergrowth to emerge in the sunlight brilliant and beautiful. A re-birth from the ashes!

EPILOGUE

The corruption and disastrous leadership in Africa has seen a never-ending cycle of violence and socio-economic collapse. States have become useless and incapable of serving their citizens many of whom are severely stressed and have to endlessly struggle for survival. Who would have guessed that the prosperous suburbs of Harare would be without drinking water, taps completely dry and sewage seeping into waterways? Incredibly many of the soul-devouring politicians in Zanu-PF have doctorates from renowned international universities, yet behave as if they are supreme dark lords who believe that they are infallible, and accept no criticism whatsoever. Mugabe has led Zimbabwe against the grain of African renaissance by imposing a one-party state, leadership for life, and a police and army controlled population. One could justifiably blame Mugabe for the HIV-AIDS epidemic in Zimbabwe which is currently claiming the lives of over 8,000 people a week, because he failed to take decisive action to invest in sustained community health and the preaching of protection. The major reason Zanu-PF have stayed in power for so long is to feed their unprecedented desire for self-enrichment, creating a system that is corrupt in all its facets. It is hard to imagine how this greedy tide will be stemmed in Zimbabwe given the history of miss-rule in Africa. What guarantees will the citizens of Zimbabwe have once a new ruling party is in place? Won't they also rush to line their pockets at the expense of the tax payer? Why did Britain, Europe and America confer so many honorary titles on Mugabe when right from the start he was tyrannical, being directly responsible for the massacre of thousands of innocent Ndebele people in the early 1980s? What mineral and agricultural interests does the West have and retain in Zimbabwe? Why is it that the travel ban on Mugabe is frequently broken during international meetings? It certainly seems that the picture is much more complex than that created by the Zanu-PF government alone. Zimbabwe needs healing and liberation!

**Termites build their nest during the December rains,
Vainona, Harare**

APPENDICES

Appendix 1 – Harare suburbs a) Immediately after Independence

A
Adylinn
Alexandra Park
Amby
Arcadia
Ardbennie
Ashbrittle
Aspindale Park
Athlone
Avondale
Avondale West
Avonlea

B
Ballantyne Park
Belgravia
Belvedere North
Belvedere South
Bingley
Bluff Hill,
Borrowdale
Borrowdale Brook
Borrowdale Park
Braeside

C
Carrick Creagh
Cayan
Chadcombe
Chikurubi
Chiltern Hills
Chisipite
Chizhanje
Cleveland
Colne Valley
Colray
Comet Rise
Cotswold Hills
Cranborne Park
Crowborough

D
Dawn Hill
Donnybrook
Dzivaresekwa

E
Eastlea North
Eastlea South
Eland Park
Emerald Hill
Epworth

G
Glen Lorne
Glen Norah
Graniteside
Greencroft
Greendale
Greengrove
Grey Lichen
Greystone Park
Grobbie Park
Gun Hill

H
Haig Park
Hatfield
Helensvale
Highfield
Highlands
Hillside
Hogerty Hill
Hopley
Houghton Park

I
Induna

K
Kambanji
Kambuzuma

Kensington
Kopje

L
Lewisam
Lichendale
Little Norfork
Lochinvar
Lorelei
Luna

M
Mabelreign
Mabvuku
Makabusi
Malvern
Mandara
Manresa
Marimba Park
Marlborough
Mayfield Park
Meyrick Park
Midlands
Milton Park
Monavale
Mount Pleasant
Mufakosi

N
Newlands
Northwood
Notley Vale

P
Park Meadowlands
Parktown
Philadelphia
Pomona
Prospect

Q
Queensdale
Quinnington

R
Rhodesville
Ridgeway
Rietfontein
Rolf Valley
Runniville

S
Sentosa
Sherwood Park
Southerton
St Andrews Park
St Martins
Stanbury Park
Strathaven
Stubbington Park
Sunningdale
Sunridge
Swan Lane Park

T
Tafara
Takeley Hill
The Grange
Tudely
Tynwald

U
Uplands

V
Vainona
Valencedene

W
Warren Park
Waterfalls
Westwood
Willowvale
Wilmington Park
Winchendon
Workington
Wormshill

Appendix 1— Harare Suburbs b) Later renamed

A
Adylinn
Alexandra Park
Amby
Arcadia
Ardbennie
Ashbrittle
Ashdown Park
Aspindale Park
Athlone
Avenues
Avondale
Avondale West
Avonlea

B
Ballantyne Park
Belgravia
Belvedere North
Belvedere South
Beverley
Bingley
Bluff Hill
Borrowdale
Borrowdale Brook
Borrowdale Park
Braeside
Budiriro

C
Carrick Creagh
Cayan
Chadcombe
Chikurubi
Chiltern Hills
Chisipite
Chizhanje
Colne Valley
Colray
Comet Rise
Cotswold Hills
Cranborne Park

D
Dawn Hill
Dzivaresekwa

E
Eastlea North
Eastlea South
Eland Park
Emerald Hill
Epworth

G
Glenhill
Glen Lorne
Glen Norah
Glen View
Grange (The)
Graniteside
Greencroft
Greendale
Greengrove
Grey Lichen
Greystone Park
Grobbie Park
Groombridge
Gunhill

H
Haig Park
Harare (City Centre)
Hatfield
Hatcliffe
Helensvale
Highfield
Highlands
Hillside
Hogerty Hill
Hopley
Houghton Park

I
Induna

K
Kambanji
Kambuzuma
Kensington
Kopje
Kuwadzana

L
Lewisam
Lichendale
Lincoln Green
Little Norfolk
Lochinvar
Logan Park
Lorelei
Luna

M
Mabelreign
Mabvuku
Malvern
Mandara
Manresa
Marlborough
Marimba Park
Mayfield Park
Mbare
Meyrick Park
Midlands
Milton Park
Monavale
Mount Pleasant
Msasa
Mufakose
Mukuvisi

N
Newlands
Northwood
Notley Vale

O
Oval Park

P
Park Meadowlands
Parktown
Philadelphia
Pomona
Prospect

Q
Queensdale
Quinnington

R
Rhodesville
Ridgeview
Rietfontein
Rolf Valley
Rugare
Runniville

S
St. Andrews Park
St. Martin's
Sandringham Park
Sentosa
Sherwood Park
Southerton
Stanbury Park
Strathaven
Sturrington
Sunningdale
Sunridge
Swan Lake Park

T
Tafara
Takeley Hill
Tudely
Tynwald

U
Uplands

V
Vainona
Valencedene

W
Warren Park
Warren Park D
Waterfalls
Westwood
Willowvale
Wilmington Park
Winchendon
Workington
Wormshill

Appendix 2 – Reserve Bank of Zimbabwe Bank Note Issues at
Independence, April 1980

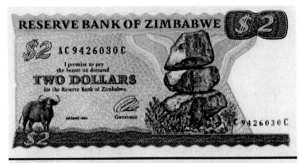

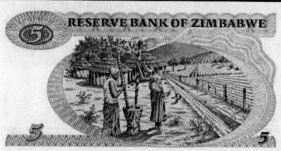

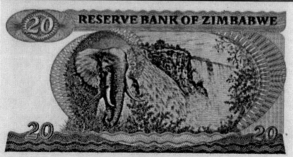

Appendix 3 – Reserve Bank of Rhodesia Bank Note Issues

Appendix 4 – An example of hyper-inflation in Zimbabwe

Permissions statement

All information in this book of a factual and historical nature, plus maps and photographs including those of the Rhodesian and Zimbabwean dollars, were obtained with permission. All information relating to the images were written in the author's own words. Other images and photographs are owned by the author. Selected sources included:

Pamwe Chete
Rhodesian's Worldwide
The Chronicle
The Fingaz
The Herald
The Zimbabwean Situation
World Health Organisation

Lightning Source UK Ltd.
Milton Keynes UK
UKOW041634080313

207357UK00001B/176/P